United Nations
Educational, Scientific and
Cultural Organization

Maritime Greenwich
inscribed on the World
Heritage List in 1997

Maritime Greenwich

Guidebook

First published in 2019 by the National Maritime Museum, Park Row, Greenwich, London SE10 9NF. This edition published in 2022.

9781906367596

Text © National Maritime Museum, London (2019)
Original text by John Bold and Charlotte Bradbeer and Pieter van der Merwe (1999)

Designed by Louise Turpin
All images © National Maritime Museum, except the following pages: 29 © James Brittain, 63 © The Fan Museum; 66 © James Keates and Trinity Laban; 79 © Royal Parks. Map design by fitcreative.ltd.uk

A CIP catalogue record for this book is available from the British Library.

Printed and bound in the UK by Belmont Press
10 9 8 7 6 5 4 3 2

This guidebook is regularly updated but please note that visitor information is liable to change.

UNESCO
United Nations Educational, Scientific and Cultural Organization

Maritime Greenwich
inscribed on the World Heritage List in 1997

FSC
www.fsc.org
MIX
Paper from responsible sources
FSC® C015185

ROYAL MUSEUMS GREENWICH

Contents

The King William Quadrangle of Greenwich Hospital, painted by James Holland, c.1850.

Introduction

Welcome to Maritime Greenwich, inscribed as a World Heritage Site by UNESCO in 1997. There are more than 1,000 such sites in over 160 countries globally. Some are natural wonders, others are man-made, but all have this international status because of their importance and outstanding universal value.

Maritime Greenwich includes the historic town centre and Greenwich Park, the Old Royal Naval College, St Alfege Church, Ranger's House and the four sites of Royal Museums Greenwich: the National Maritime Museum, Royal Observatory, *Cutty Sark* and the Queen's House. Many of the buildings were designed by the greatest British architects of the 17th and 18th centuries, and as a group they form a unique historic townscape.

Greenwich was the site of a major royal palace from the mid-15th century and both Henry VIII and Elizabeth I were born here. From 1676 Charles II's Royal Observatory made it a centre of pioneering work for the improvement of navigation and global time-keeping. The Royal Hospital for Seamen, begun in 1696, was a national institution for maritime welfare before it became the home of the Royal Naval College (1873–1998), and today it is a popular attraction, as well as home to the University of Greenwich and Trinity Laban Conservatoire of Music and Dance. Greenwich was therefore the ideal site for the National Maritime Museum, opened in 1937, and for the preservation of *Cutty Sark*, the last and most famous of the tea clippers, which arrived in 1954 and opened to the public in 1957.

All this and much more is here for you to enjoy.

Did you know?

The story of the World Heritage Site is briefly told in the Visitor Centre at the Old Royal Naval College. You can also get more information about Greenwich at the Greenwich Tourist Information desk there.

Greenwich through time

1426: Humphrey, Duke of Gloucester, inherits the manor at Greenwich and later starts work on a riverside house.

1533: Princess Elizabeth, later Elizabeth I, is born at Greenwich Palace.

1616: Anne of Denmark, wife of James I, commissions architect Inigo Jones to build the Queen's House.

c.1638: The Queen's House is completed during the reign of Charles I for his wife Henrietta Maria.

1447: Humphrey's manor returns to the Crown, and develops as Greenwich Palace. In Henry VIII's reign (1485–1509) it becomes the principal Tudor palace.

1491: Prince Henry, later Henry VIII, is born at Greenwich Palace.

1675: Charles II commissions Christopher Wren to build the Royal Observatory at Greenwich 'for perfecting the art of navigation'.

1694: King William and Queen Mary issue a royal charter for the founding of Greenwich Hospital for 'the relief and support of seamen'. It closes in 1869.

1712–15: Greenwich Hospital School is founded for 'the maintenance and education of the children of seamen'. The school remains at Greenwich until 1933.

1884: The Greenwich Meridian, defined by the Royal Observatory, is adopted as the Prime Meridian of the World (0° longitude).

1937: The National Maritime Museum opens in the former Greenwich Hospital School buildings, including the Queen's House.

1997: Maritime Greenwich is designated a World Heritage Site by the United Nations Educational, Scientific and Cultural Organization (UNESCO).

1873: The Royal Naval College, Portsmouth, moves into the former Greenwich Hospital buildings. The college moves out in 1998.

1954: The clipper *Cutty Sark* is moved to dry dock at Greenwich. It opens to the public three years later.

2012: The London 2012 Olympics equestrian events take place in Greenwich Park.

▼ Greenwich Hospital, painted by Canaletto around the time of its completion in 1751, with the Queen's House, Greenwich Park and Royal Observatory in the background.

History of Greenwich

On Thames's bank in silent thought we stood,
Where Greenwich smiles upon the silver flood;
Struck with the seat that gave Eliza birth,
We kneel, and kiss the consecrated earth.

Dr Samuel Johnson

When Dr Johnson wrote this in 1738, a year after living there, Greenwich was a riverside village on the fringe of London, and already had a long history. Strategically placed next to the main land and water routes from continental Europe to the capital, it was one of the main bases for the Danish conquest of England in the early 11th century. The site of a small Roman shrine on the east side of the Park and a cluster of Anglo-Saxon burial mounds on the west show even older occupation.

In Johnson's time, Greenwich's main activities were centred on the Royal Naval Hospital, founded in 1694 and completed in 1751. This replaced the former royal palace where King Henry VIII and Queen Elizabeth I were born, and of which Inigo Jones's Queen's House (1616–c.1638), is the only surviving building. The Hospital was home to the blue-coated and battle-scarred Pensioners of the Royal Navy until 1869. It then served as the Royal Naval College from 1873 and also as the Joint Services Defence College from 1983, both for advanced officer training, before they moved to Wiltshire in 1998.

These Thames-side buildings, with the Royal Observatory crowning the first of London's royal parks behind them, form the finest architectural landscape in Britain. The Observatory itself was founded by Charles II in 1675, expressly to improve the seaborne navigation on which the wealth and security of Britain depended. It did this by accurately mapping the stars, for which accurate time measurement was critical: since 1884 the world has also set its clocks according to time on

▶ *'H4', John Harrison's prizewinning timekeeper of 1759, which finally solved the problem of finding longitude at sea.*

▶ 'K2', Larcum Kendall's second, simplified version of Harrison's 'H4', which was issued to Lieutenant Bligh in 1787 for the ill-fated Bounty voyage.

the meridian of Greenwich, Longitude 0°, the basis of the International Time Zone system.

Nowhere else in the United Kingdom has so many outstanding buildings designed by our foremost classical architects. The town centre also bears the imprint of over 300 years of growth and adaptation, and still largely preserves the elegant Georgian domestic and commercial buildings it had gained by the 1840s. Until the Thames became badly polluted in the late 19th century, whitebait swam upriver as far as Greenwich and were a local delicacy, attracting celebrities and others to the surviving Trafalgar Tavern, and The Ship, on the spot where *Cutty Sark* now stands in dry-dock.

Though its royal and other famous inhabitants have gone, they would still easily recognise the Park, the great buildings and the bustling urban scene. The river, now much cleaner, is busy once again. Historic Greenwich has largely survived: an island in the city, where the story of Britain and the sea, and of time itself, can be enjoyed in a unique architectural and landscape setting.

Royal Greenwich

Greenwich has had royal connections for 600 years, a history celebrated in 2012, when it formally became a Royal Borough to mark HM The Queen's Diamond Jubilee. There was a royal manor in Greenwich from at least the 15th century, when a new Thames-side house called Bellacourt was built here by Humphrey, Duke of Gloucester, regent to his nephew, the young King Henry VI, from 1426. In 1433 Humphrey fenced in 200 acres (81 hectares) of heath and woodland to form the Park, and built a watchtower where the Observatory now stands. After his death in 1447, Bellacourt passed to Margaret of Anjou, wife of Henry VI, and was renamed Placentia, while 'Duke Humphrey's Tower' was later remodelled as a lodge by Henry VIII, who housed one of his mistresses there.

Placentia was largely rebuilt by Henry VII around 1500 and became the Palace of Greenwich. Until the building of Whitehall Palace in the 1530s, it was a principal Crown residence, as the first (or last) port of call for visiting ambassadors from mainland Europe. Henry VIII, a compulsive builder and an enthusiastic horseman and jouster, made further alterations during his reign (1509–47). He redesigned the chapel, remodelled stables and added a tiltyard with towers and a viewing gallery. Martial displays, in which he played a vigorous part, became highlights of diplomatic and other such events, marked by jousts, banqueting, the performance of masques and dancing until dawn. It was also here that Henry established his armoury (the first of its kind in England) and his two great naval dockyards nearby – at Woolwich to the east and Deptford to the west.

▲ ▶ *Portraits of Henry VIII and Elizabeth I. Both Henry and Elizabeth were born in the palace at Greenwich and used it as a main residence.*

When Whitehall replaced it as the leading seat of Tudor government, Greenwich became a royal country retreat. Henry VIII's daughter Elizabeth I, who spent most summers here, maintained the banqueting houses and added a new one in 1559, but did little other building. Under King James I, the courtier Earl of Northampton revamped Duke Humphrey's Tower as the ornamental castle of Millefleur, complete with a kitchen, wine cellar and private garden. At the same time James I replaced the fence around the Park with a brick wall approximately 2 miles (3.2 km) in length and 12 feet (3.5 m) high, at a cost of about £2,000. In the Palace, he added a stone-vaulted undercroft beneath the Great Hall and built new lodgings for his wife, Anne of Denmark.

Shortly afterwards he assigned the Palace to Anne, and she began improvements, among which was her greatly admired Italianate garden.

Devised by the French garden designer and hydraulic engineer, Salomon de Caus, the garden had fountains, water-pouring statues, an aviary and a shell-encrusted grotto. Anne's final innovation was to have Inigo Jones design the Queen's House in 1616, overlooking the gardens. Building stopped before she died in 1619 and it was ten years before her daughter-in-law Queen Henrietta Maria resumed it, reviving the gardens and completing the House by about 1638.

After the Restoration of King Charles II in 1660, the dilapidated Palace of Greenwich was gradually demolished as part of his plan to replace it with a modern classical structure of three wings, with the river on the fourth side. This was designed by John Webb, a pupil of Inigo Jones, but financial difficulties meant that only the west range was begun in 1664. Boarded up in 1669, still incomplete, it was used as a gunpowder store until Queen Mary II decided to incorporate it into her new hospital for seamen in 1694.

Charles's intentions for the Park were comparably ambitious. A plan prepared by the great French garden designer, André le Nôtre, creator of the park at Versailles, was, however, only partly executed. It was mainly implemented by Sir William Boreman, who planted many of the tree-lined avenues and, in 1661–62, cut the Giant Steps that linked the upper and lower parts of the Park. Traces of these are still visible on the eroded central slope up to the Observatory. At the south end of the Park, the major and minor avenues radiated from a semicircle of trees flanked by contrived wildernesses, one of which – the Great Wilderness – survives as a small area of woodland. Henry VIII first introduced deer to the Park in 1515–18, and they ran free until 1927.

The Queen's House

Designed by Inigo Jones, this Italianate 'house of delight' is one of the most important buildings in British architectural history, representing the pure classicism that Jones introduced to England. Today it displays a superb art collection.

rmg.co.uk/queens-house

10.00–17.00 Mon–Sun

Free entry and audio tour; ticketed tours

The Queen's House was designed in 1616 for James I's queen, Anne of Denmark (1574–1619), but building stopped in 1618 when it was only one storey high. Queen Henrietta Maria (1609–69), wife of King Charles I, resumed construction after 1629 and was still engaged on lavish interior furnishing at the start of the Civil War in 1642, which destroyed the Stuart idyll, resulting in the King's execution and the Queen living in exile until 1662.

The House was created by Inigo Jones as a small-scale version of a Renaissance villa, and as a private retreat for the Stuart queens, based on extensive study of architecture and gardens in Italy. His specific model was the Medici villa at Poggio a Caiano, outside Florence, by Giuliano da Sangallo. Instead of Sangallo's central salon, however, Jones designed the House as an H-block with a central bridge over the old Deptford to Woolwich road, which then divided the palace gardens from the Park. At the time it was regarded as a 'curious device' (i.e. an intriguing creation). In the 1660s the upper floor was altered to a more conventional, fully connected square layout with the

▼ *Inigo Jones (1573–1652). Little is known of Jones before he gained fame as a designer of court masques.*

▼ *Anne of Denmark (1572–1619), James I's queen, in a portrait by John de Critz.*

addition of two further bridge rooms, creating 'king's side' and 'queen's side' apartments that partly obscure the original H-plan. The road beneath was moved north to its present position in about 1699.

The House has had a chequered history, remaining in the ownership of the Crown but occupied by various people including the Ranger of Greenwich Park, a post held in the early 18th century by the Governor of the Royal Hospital (to 1743). It was also used as a place for receiving royal visitors to England, including George, Elector of Hanover, before his coronation as George I in 1714, and a number of later royal brides. From the early 19th century it housed the Greenwich (later Royal) Hospital School, before being restored from 1934 as centrepiece of the new National Maritime Museum. The House was partly used for naval purposes during the Second World War, notably by the Women's Royal Naval Service (WRNS).

The cubic, galleried hall, the dramatic Tulip Stairs and the mid-17th century plasterwork of the east and west bridge rooms, as well as the view of the

▶ The south façade was the front of the House when first designed. Its first-floor loggia provides an elevated view over the Park.

▲ Van Dyck studio portraits of
Henrietta Maria and her husband,
Charles I.

▶ The Tulip Stairs was the first self-supporting
spiral staircase in Britain. Its name derives
from the painted tulip pattern on the wrought-
iron balustrade.

Park from the loggia, give a flavour of the grandeur intended by the royal
occupants. Much of the decorative painting commissioned by Henrietta Maria
remained incomplete, however, and many artworks that were installed were
dispersed after the execution of Charles I in 1649. The original ceiling paintings
in the Great Hall, forming an 'Allegory of Peace and the Arts under the
English Crown' were by Orazio Gentileschi, probably helped by his daughter
Artemisia, who oversaw their installation after his death. They were removed
to Marlborough House, Westminster, in about 1708 but the Queen's Presence
Chamber still has the original 1630s ceiling coving painted in 'grotesque-work'.

Today the Queen's House is one of the four sites that comprise Royal
Museums Greenwich, and displays some of the superb art collection of the
National Maritime Museum. Through its style, position and status, the House
also determined the form of all later developments on the Greenwich site,
including the 'Grand Axis' from the river up through the Park. When it was
built, the House had no view to or from the Thames, and only gained one with
the demolition of the older palace buildings in the 1670s. Both Charles II's plans

for a new palace and Sir Christopher Wren's original design for the Royal Hospital would have blocked the view again, but this was stopped by Queen Mary II: in founding the Hospital, she reserved a strip of ground, the width of the House, to form a vista to the river. Captain Sir William Gifford, the first Governor of the Hospital, was an early beneficiary: in 1712 he ordered two oak seats for the terrace, from which to enjoy the view.

A major renovation of the Queen's House was completed in 2016 to commemorate its 400th anniversary. This provided an opportunity for the Turner Prize-winning artist Richard Wright to produce a site-specific piece on the ceiling of the Great Hall – the first living artist to do so since the 17th century. The acquisition of the 'Armada Portrait' of Elizabeth I has further reinforced the focus of displays in the House on the lives and accomplishments of British queens.

Displayed alongside the historic fine art holdings are contemporary artworks that engage with these and the history of the House itself. Recent acquisitions include Kehinde Wiley's *Ship of Fools*, the first work by this African-American painter to enter a British public collection, as well as numerous other paintings, prints and photographs by other contemporary artists.

Henrietta Maria's 'house of delight' was imagined as a space to enjoy both new and historic artworks, music and other performance. The present-day Queen's House maintains those traditions nearly 400 years later.

◀ *(Previous page) The grotesque ceiling in the Queen's Presence Chamber is probably by Edward Pearce, who worked on other schemes with Jones, and based on French patterns. The central panel of 'Aurora dispersing the shades of night' is later.*

▲ *The iconic 'Armada Portrait' of Elizabeth I commemorates the most famous conflict of her reign – the failed invasion of England by the Spanish Armada in 1588. It was acquired for the nation in 2016 following a joint appeal by Royal Museums Greenwich and the Art Fund.*

Old Royal Naval College

An outstanding complex of baroque buildings, built between 1696 and 1751 and designed primarily by Sir Christopher Wren and Nicholas Hawksmoor. Originally constructed as the Royal Hospital for Seamen, the buildings then housed the Royal Naval College (1873–1998) and are now home to the Painted Hall, Visitor Centre and Chapel, as well as the University of Greenwich and the Trinity Laban Conservatoire of Music and Dance.

🌐 ornc.org

🕐 10.00–17.00 Mon–Sun
Grounds open 08.00-23.00

🎟 Visitor Centre, Chapel and grounds free. Charged admission to Painted Hall

▲ *The twin domes of the Old Royal Naval College, seen from the south end of Upper Grand Square.*

The College is the finest piece of monumental classical architecture in England, and holds two masterpieces of interior decoration: Sir James Thornhill's baroque Painted Hall and the neoclassical chapel. The Old Royal Naval College stands on the site of the former Tudor Palace of Greenwich. Its earliest visible section is the east side of the King Charles Court, which

Hidden gem

Look out for Joshua Marshall's carvings (1660s) in the east and north pediments of the King Charles building, which show the royal Stuart arms supported respectively by figures of Fortitude and Dominion of the Seas, and by Mars and Fame.

was the start of a new palace for Charles II in the 1660s. When Queen Mary II decided that this and the rest of the site be 'converted and employed as a hospital for seamen', she also decreed that the Queen's House retain a view to the river, hence the unusual arrangement of paired buildings each side of a central vista. She died of smallpox in December 1694 and her husband William III continued the project in her memory, promising an endowment of £2,000 a year. Sir Christopher Wren, formally appointed Surveyor in 1696, worked free of charge. Assisted by Nicholas Hawksmoor, who in 1698 became Clerk of Works, and by John James, assistant to Hawksmoor from 1705 and later joint Clerk, Wren laid out the main lines of the Hospital, including all of the foundations. The 'courts' were designed by Wren and Hawksmoor with the exception of the last, the Queen Mary Court, although this outwardly mirrors its domed Wren 'pair' (King William Court).

Despite the promising start, the project was bedevilled by financial difficulties, with construction spread across four main phases between 1696 and 1751, and further improvements made into the 19th century. By 1699 the scheme was £9,000 in debt, growing to £19,000 by 1702. It was only in 1735, when the Hospital was granted the northern estates of the Earl of Derwentwater (who was executed for supporting the Jacobite rising of 1715), that it gained the steady income which allowed Thomas Ripley, a reliable rather than outstanding architect, to begin the Queen Mary Court. Given the problems, it is remarkable that the Hospital was completed at all, let alone in such splendid style.

Queen Mary founded the Hospital with what Hawksmoor called a 'fixt Intention for Magnificence'. Although such residential hospitals primarily aimed to fulfil the welfare obligations of monarchs to support men disabled in serving their country, they were also intended as symbols of state power, wealth and benevolence. Given Britain's role as a leading maritime power, building her Royal Naval Hospital on the river highway connecting London with the world was as much a political as a philanthropic act. This was highlighted by the spectacular decorative scheme in the Painted Hall, which launched Greenwich as an international visitor attraction from 1712, when Thornhill finished the main ceiling. The voluntary charge to view it was soon made compulsory, and from about 1715 allowed the Hospital to found what eventually became the Royal Hospital School for the sons of seamen: this still exists (for boys and girls) at Holbrook, Suffolk, after leaving Greenwich in 1933.

The Painted Hall

The Painted Hall houses the finest example of baroque decorative painting by an English artist. Sir James Thornhill's ceiling, 1708–12, celebrates the triumph of Protestant monarchy: William and Mary, attended by the Virtues, Concord and Peace, present the cap of liberty to Europe above the crouching figure of tyranny, in the form of Louis XIV of France. The Upper Hall decoration, 1718–25, shows (on the ceiling) Mary's sister Queen Anne and her husband, Prince George of Denmark, while the Royal family of George I presides over Naval Victory, Peace and Plenty on the end wall. In 1824, the Painted Hall became the 'National Gallery of Naval Art' (or Naval Gallery), eventually housing over 300 donated paintings and attracting thousands of visitors a year. It lasted until 1936 when its holdings passed into the care of the newly founded National Maritime Museum and became known as the Greenwich Hospital Collection. The Painted Hall has seen many restorations, most recently a complete conservation project, bringing its magnificent interior vividly back to life. As part of these works, the Undercroft beneath the Painted Hall was renovated and now houses a café, shop and interpretation gallery, alongside a visible section of the foundations of Greenwich Palace, which were uncovered at the same time.

Did you know?

The neoclassical chapel in the Queen Mary Building was rebuilt by James 'Athenian' Stuart and William Newton after the original interior was gutted by a fire in 1779. It is Stuart's late masterpiece in the Greek-revival style.

Hidden gem

In the colonnade pediment in the King William building, Benjamin West's Coade-stone sculpture of 1810–12 commemorates the battles and death of Nelson. It measures 12 × 50 feet and the Coade factory considered it their greatest work.

The Painted Hall was originally intended as the Hospital dining hall, its officers using the Upper Hall at the west end.

The Royal Hospital for Seamen

'Greenwich Hospital' was for Royal Naval seamen who were unable to maintain themselves due to age or disability. The first Greenwich Pensioners arrived in 1705 and there were 1,000 by 1738. At its peak, in 1814, the Hospital housed 2,710 'in-Pensioners', with several thousand others who (from 1763) drew 'out-Pensions' to support themselves either locally or elsewhere. The original capacity of the buildings was expanded, particularly in the more space-efficient Queen Mary Court (1735–51). Construction of a dedicated infirmary in the 1760s (now the Dreadnought Building) also made more space during a period of worldwide naval conflict.

With such large numbers, two sittings for meals were needed in the two colonnaded dining rooms (each with its own kitchen) beneath the Chapel and Painted Hall. Smoking was limited to specific places, such as the Chalk Walk, a long basement under the east colonnade, which eventually became a skittle alley. A Pensioners' library was added in 1828 but otherwise there was little in the form of entertainment for these disabled sailors. Demand for places declined in a long mid-19th-century era of naval peace, and the Hospital eventually closed, with the final Pensioners leaving in 1869. Greenwich Hospital however continues to this day as a Royal Naval Crown Charity supporting serving and retired personnel of the Royal Naval Service.

Royal Naval College

In 1873 the Admiralty moved its Naval College from Portsmouth to form the Royal Naval College at Greenwich, 'for the education of officers of all ranks above midshipman'. In 1983 the Joint Services Defence College also transferred here. In 1998, following the Government's decision to move these

Did you know?

The Pensioners' diet was plain and repetitive: mutton on two days a week, beef on three, with pea soup and cheese on the other two. Two quarts of beer a day were provided, which were piped to the dining areas from the Hospital's own brewhouse.

service training facilities elsewhere, responsibility for the College passed to the Greenwich Foundation, whose overall responsibility is for the College, the Painted Hall, the Chapel and the grounds. The main buildings are now occupied by the University of Greenwich, and the King Charles Court by Trinity Laban Conservatoire of Music and Dance.

Pepys Building

Erected between 1874 and 1883, this was originally the Royal Naval College's fives and racquets courts, flanking an open central courtyard. The court was roofed over as an engineering laboratory around 1906. The building is notable for its imposing river façade, inset with busts of British naval heroes. It now holds the visitor centre for the World Heritage Site and Old Royal Naval College, the Greenwich Tourist Information Centre and the Old Brewery pub. The former Hospital stable block between the Pepys Building and the West Gate was built by Joseph Kay in 1836 and was at that time outside the Hospital grounds.

▼ Officers Dining in the Painted Hall during the Second World War, *by Sir Muirhead Bone. WRNS officers are seated at the centre table, some of the first women ever to dine in the Painted Hall.*

Royal Observatory

The Royal Observatory is made up of Flamsteed House, the Meridian and Great Equatorial Buildings, the Altazimuth Pavilion and South Building, which is now home to the Astronomy Centre and Peter Harrison Planetarium. It is also the home of the Prime Meridian and Greenwich Mean Time (GMT).

rmg.co.uk/royal-observatory

10.00–17.00 Mon–Sun

Charged admission; free audio tour

▶ *Flamsteed House, the original Royal Observatory building, constructed in 1675–76. The low extension to the left replaced an earlier one in the 1830s.*

◀ *John Flamsteed, from a portrait by Thomas Gibson. Born in 1646, Flamsteed was appointed the first Astronomer Royal at Greenwich in 1675.*

Since 1884, the world has set its clocks according to the time of day on the meridian of Greenwich, Longitude 0°, which is defined by the Airy Transit Circle installed at the Royal Observatory in 1850–51. This was a development from the Observatory's original purpose, which was set out when Charles II appointed John Flamsteed as his first Astronomer Royal in 1675, instructing him, 'to apply himself with the most exact care and diligence to the rectifying of the tables of the motions of the heavens, and the places of the fixed stars, so as to find out the so much-desired longitude of places for perfecting the art of navigation'. At that time Britain was a rising sea power, and finding accurate longitude (east–west position) in mid-ocean was the greatest of many navigational problems. It would remain so for over 80 years, since it could only be done by accurate time measurement. North and south position (latitude) was relatively easy to find by observation; but instrumentation and charts also needed improvement and all required accurate celestial data.

Flamsteed House

Flamsteed House is the original Observatory building, built in 1675–76 by Sir Christopher Wren with the help of Robert Hooke, on the foundations of Duke Humphrey's Tower/Greenwich Castle. The site had the advantages of being on then-secluded royal ground, near to London but outside its smoky haze, and also high up with clear fields of view.

Flamsteed House had domestic accommodation on the lower floors to house the Astronomers Royal and their families, with the Star Room, now called the Octagon Room, above it. This was large and grand enough to welcome VIPs, and to accommodate long telescopes and two specialised clocks. These were built for Flamsteed by Thomas Tompion and installed in 1676, each with a 13-foot (4 m) pendulum for accurate time-reckoning. They required winding only once a year and enabled Flamsteed to establish that the Earth rotated at an even rate, giving him a basis for precisely charting the stars by timed observations of their transit (crossing a meridian) over his head.

Meridian and Great Equatorial Buildings

The present Meridian Building grew from an originally small brick shed to the south of Flamsteed House. Here Flamsteed mounted his transit quadrant on a wall that ran truly north–south and first defined a 'Greenwich Meridian'. The official meridian moved east four times as subsequent Astronomers Royal set up ever more accurate transit instruments in eastward extensions of what is now the Meridian Building, coming to rest on the line of Airy's Transit Circle. The roof above this great instrument still opens to allow observation.

The octagonal Great Equatorial Building was added in 1857 as a telescope tower, now bearing an onion dome covering the 28-inch (71 cm) refracting telescope of 1894, still the world's eighth largest. The Victorian dome was removed in 1953 after being damaged in 1944 by a near miss from a V1 flying bomb. It was replaced in 1975 with a fibreglass replica.

◀ *The Octagon Room (shown as now and originally), was first called the 'Star Room'. The engraving by Francis Place (1676) shows the first Astronomer Royal, John Flamsteed, and his two assistants at work.*

The Altazimuth Pavilion and South Building

These buildings were both erected in 1894–99. The Pavilion originally held a telescope on an altazimuth mounting, enabling movement on both north–south (altitude) and east–west (azimuth) axes. In 2018, following a successful appeal, a suite of research-grade telescopes was installed in the Altazimuth Pavilion's restored dome, equipped with computer-controlled systems, digital cameras and filters to limit the effect of light pollution, so that the night sky can again be brought to visitors to the site and online. Collectively called the Annie Maunder Astrographic Telescope or AMAT (named after one of the first women to work at the Observatory), this has made Greenwich a working observatory again for the first time in 60 years. The much larger South Building, originally the 'New Physical Observatory', was built in phases to 1899 and reopened in May 2007 as a public astronomy centre, after total internal remodelling. The centre also includes the striking 120-seat Peter Harrison Planetarium, under a raised courtyard and truncated bronze cone. The design of the cone takes into account its location in relation to the zenith, the north celestial pole, the celestial equator and the meridian.

Altazimuth Pavilion

Modern astronomy

City pollution, the building of Greenwich Power Station in 1902–10, and the disturbing effects of electric railways on magnetic observations, obliged the Observatory to move aspects of its work elsewhere from the 1920s. The Second World War accelerated this and, afterwards, all scientific work moved to Herstmonceux in Sussex. The last Astronomer Royal at Greenwich left in 1948, although positional observations continued here until 1954, a year after the buildings were allocated to the National Maritime Museum and became known as the Old Royal Observatory. In July 1960, Queen Elizabeth II opened the restored Flamsteed House, with the complex being fully reopened to the public in 1967. In 1998, the Royal Observatory, Greenwich, reassumed its original title and an expanded educational role in modern astronomy.

▲ The north exteriors of the Meridian Building and the Great Equatorial Building overlook the Meridian Courtyard.

◀ The Altazimuth Pavilion, 1899, with its still-functioning telescope dome, now holds the Annie Maunder Astrographic Telescope, named after this pioneering female astronomer and astrophotographer.

National Maritime Museum

The National Maritime Museum (NMM) is the world's largest maritime museum, telling stories of Britain's epic relationship with the sea. It also contains the Caird Library, the largest maritime historical library and archive in the world, with some items dating back to the 15th century.

 rmg.co.uk/national-maritime-museum

 10.00–17.00 Mon–Sun

 Free admission and audio tour. Charged entry to special exhibitions, events and daily tours.

▲ The Kongouro from New Holland (Kangaroo) *and* Portrait of a Large Dog, *by George Stubbs. 'Kangaroo' and 'Dingo' were commissioned by Sir Joseph Banks (1743–1820), following his participation on Captain James Cook's first voyage to the Pacific (1768–71). These two works are part of the extensive collection of oil paintings in the National Maritime Museum.*

The National Maritime Museum is the flagship of Royal Museums Greenwich, and its seafaring collections are unequalled in terms of both quality and size. It tells the story of global encounters, cultural exchange and human endurance, and includes the world's finest collection on the Royal Navy in the era of sail, and in particular on Nelson and his times.

There are over 2.6 million items in the collection, though only a small proportion can be shown at any time. This includes more than

- 100,000 books
- 397,500 items in the manuscripts collection
- 90,000 sea charts
- 4,000 oil paintings
- 70,000 prints and drawings
- 1 million ship plans
- up to 1 million historic photographs
- 280,000 negatives
- 44,500 3-D objects, including small craft, ship models, coins and medals, decorative art, figureheads, relics, horological instruments, uniforms and weapons.

The Museum was founded by Act of Parliament in 1934, and opened in the Queen's House and adjoining buildings in 1937.

History of the Museum buildings

The two inner wings were added to the Queen's House in 1807–11 to convert it into a school – the Royal Naval Asylum. This was established at Greenwich by Royal Warrant in 1805 to accommodate 700 boys and (until 1841) 300 girls. The architect of these extensions was Daniel Asher Alexander 'in strict accordance with the style of Inigo Jones'. He produced a very sympathetic result, including the colonnades that served as play areas for the children.

The Asylum was taken over by Greenwich Hospital from 1821. Combined with the previously separate Greenwich Hospital School, which educated 'orphans of the sea' from 1715, they became respectively the Lower and Upper Schools of Greenwich Hospital. After organisational reform, for boys only from 1841, the buildings were extended with a south and outer west wing in 1861–62, designed by Philip Charles Hardwick. In 1873 an iron-vaulted gymnasium known as 'Neptune's Hall' was added between the two west wings, behind the imposing Doric façade that now forms the NMM's north entrance. A large dining hall and dormitory wing were the final additions on the west side in 1876, and the whole complex was renamed the Royal Hospital School in 1892.

After the school moved out to Suffolk in 1933, the buildings were converted to house the new Museum, largely at the cost of Sir James Caird (1864–1954), a Scottish ship owner who was its greatest early benefactor. He put over £1.25 million (well over £150 million in today's terms) into acquisitions and building alterations, working with its Trustees and first Director, Sir Geoffrey Callender. During the conversion a top-lit rotunda by Sir Edwin Lutyens was inserted into its west wing, honouring Sir James. The Greenwich Hospital Collection of paintings, displayed in the Painted Hall of the Royal Naval College, and material from the former Royal Naval Museum there, were transferred to the new Museum's care in 1936.

Redevelopment

Neptune's Hall was used for the royal opening by King George VI in 1937, and afterwards became a display area for boats, models and other large objects until 1972, when it was redesigned as the new 'Neptune Hall'. In 1996–99, the Hall was replaced by Neptune Court – the vast atrium which forms the centre of today's Museum, beneath the glass and steel roof that spans the whole area between the flanking 19th-century west wings.

In 2011, HRH The Duke of Edinburgh, the Museum's Patron, opened the new Sammy Ofer Wing. A major part of its cost was met by the largest single benefaction yet given to a British museum; a £20-million donation from Sammy Ofer. Born in Romania, he had served in the Royal Navy during the Second World War and later built up an international shipping business. The Portland-stone extension holds an 8,610 sq. foot (800 m²) international-standard special exhibition gallery at basement level, as well as a café and terrace. Additionally, a complete internal conversion of the adjacent south-west wing of 1876 changed three floors into four, to hold a new gallery at ground level below an enlarged, modern reading room for the Caird Library, and two-and-a-half floors of library and archive storage space above.

In 2018 four new galleries were added in what was formerly the old Caird Library and office space above in the old central west wing of 1807–11: 'Tudor and Stuart Seafarers', 'Pacific Encounters', 'Polar Worlds', and 'Sea Things'. This has provided easy public circulation on all three floors around the central Neptune Court and the new display of over 1,100 additional objects relating to seaborne exploration from the 16th to 20th centuries.

◀ *The Royal Opening of the National Maritime Museum by King George VI, 1937.*

▶ Nelson's Ship in a Bottle, *by Yinka Shonibare, CBE; a 1:30 replica of HMS Victory, acquired by the National Maritime Museum after a successful public appeal and a generous grant from the Art Fund.*

Cutty Sark *statistics*
Tonnage: 963 tons
Sail area: 32,000 sq. ft. (2,987 m²)
Best day's run: 363 nautical miles
Highest measured speed: 17.5 knots

Cutty Sark

Built in 1869 and now the world's sole-surviving tea clipper, Cutty Sark's iron-framed teak hull has now been raised over three metres, allowing visitors the jaw-dropping experience of walking directly underneath its keel to appreciate the spectacular underwater lines that made it the fastest ship of its time.

 rmg.co.uk/cutty-sark

 10.00–17.00 Mon–Sun

 Charged admission; free audio tour

This beautiful tea clipper, the fastest ship of its time and the last survivor of its type, is preserved in dry-dock as a tribute to the ships and men of the Merchant Navy in the days of sail, and as a testimony to London's distinguished maritime past. Built of teak on an iron frame by Scott and Linton, *Cutty Sark* was launched at Dumbarton in Scotland in 1869. Ironically, the same year saw the opening the Suez Canal, which spelt the end of the high-value sailing trade in tea for which *Cutty Sark* was built. The ship's fastest passages, on which it really made its name, were in the Australian wool trade, to which it turned after 1877, principally under the command of Captain Richard Woodget between 1885 and 1895. Immensely strong and powerful, the ship was famous for overhauling both sailing and steam vessels, the most celebrated of many occasions being in 1889, when it overtook the new P&O mail steamer *Britannia* on the run into Sydney. On Woodget's first voyage in 1885, *Cutty Sark* defeated its old tea-trade rival *Thermopylae* on the voyage from Sydney by a full week, arriving off the coast of Kent after 73 days at sea.

From 1895 *Cutty Sark* was in Portuguese ownership as the *Ferreira*, but was bought back in 1922 by Captain Wilfred Dowman of Falmouth. In 1938 the ship was brought to Greenhithe on the lower Thames as a training ship for the Thames Nautical Training College. When no longer needed for this purpose, the Cutty Sark Preservation Society, formed in 1952, ensured its survival. The ship was moored off Deptford as part of the Festival of Britain in 1951. In 1954 it was moved into its specially built dry-dock, and after three years of restoration was opened to the public by HM The Queen.

> **Did you know?**
>
> *2019 marked Cutty Sark's 150th anniversary. Having been designed to last just 30 years, this is a remarkable achievement.*

▶ *Only seven clipper ships that sailed the China Seas alongside* Cutty Sark *survived into the 20th century, and by the mid-1920s* Cutty Sark *was the only one still afloat.*

25th June 1957

Opening by

HER MAJESTY THE QUEEN
of the

Cutty Sark

in her permanent berth at Greenwich

◀ *Cover of the programme of the Royal Opening of the* Cutty Sark, *25 June 1957.*

▶ *HM The Queen at the reopening of* Cutty Sark, *25 April 2012, following its major re-conservation project.*

Recent restoration

After 50 years in its Greenwich dry-dock, and despite further restoration, *Cutty Sark*'s structure had badly deteriorated as a result of rainwater ingress and complex, long-term corrosion processes in its wrought-iron frame. In November 2006 a major new conservation programme began to counter the metal decay and consolidate the wooden hull planks. In May 2007, however, a major fire badly set back the project, although with fortunately minimal loss of original fabric. When the ship reopened in 2012, it had been permanently raised over 10 feet (3 m) and surrounded by a dramatic glass canopy covering the dock. This design allows the space underneath the hull to be used for interpretation of *Cutty Sark* and its history, the display of its extensive figurehead collection (there are over 80), and for events to take place.

CUTTY SARK WAS OPENED
TO THE PUBLIC IN GREENWICH BY
HM QUEEN ELIZABETH II
ON 25th ⬦⬦⬦⬦⬦ ⬦⬦⬦⬦

CUTTY SARK WAS RE-OPENED BY
HM QUEEN ELIZABETH II
FOLLOW⬦⬦⬦ ITS ⬦⬦⬦⬦⬦ER
CONSER⬦ATION ⬦⬦⬦⬦⬦⬦⬦
ON 25th APRIL ⬦⬦⬦⬦
DURING HER MAJESTY'S DIAMOND JUBILEE

Greenwich: the Town

For centuries the River Thames was the principal and easiest route to Greenwich, and the approach by river remains equally dramatic today.

You can appreciate the full extent of the historic heart of Greenwich from a boat in mid-stream or from Island Gardens on the north bank: the eye is led from the riverside courts of the Old Royal Naval College to the central Queen's House and up to the Royal Observatory on the hill. The Five-Foot Walk across the riverfront of the

College terminates to the east with the Trafalgar Tavern and to the west with the masts of the *Cutty Sark*, standing close to where the main landing place for Greenwich has always been.

Greenwich was always a place of river workers, fishermen and seamen. From 1705, when the first naval Pensioners arrived, it also became a Royal Naval town. Wives and families of the 'in-Pensioners' came to live near their men, and Hospital 'out-Pensioners' and other seamen also settled locally. Wives took in washing or worked as servants or in shops. Pensioners, distinctive by their uniform, disabilities, seamanlike bearing and nautical speech, filled the narrow lanes, took the air in the Park and for a small coin or tobacco regaled holiday visitors with tales of great battles, exotic foreign lands, and storms and shipwrecks on distant oceans.

Greenwich was a place of inexpensive and often licentious pleasures, with its riotous twice-yearly fair (to 1857), and its pot-houses and taverns. The carved balconies of the Salutation and Peter Boat taverns hung over the landing place for many trippers coming by water from London. The original Ship tavern was also on the Thames, off narrow Fisher Lane, behind the modern pier. Pictures, stories and song celebrate the Pensioners and show

◀ The Pensioner's Story, *by Thomas Davidson (1883). A pensioner talks to visitors in Greenwich outside the King Charles Court of Greenwich Hospital, c.1810.*

them carousing in such haunts, refighting old battles over foaming tankards and long clay pipes. Their main enemy was boredom: the Hospital looked after them well, but it was strictly run and they had few occupations – not even a reading room until 1828.

The historic town now has the late-Georgian appearance given to it by Joseph Kay, then Surveyor to Greenwich Hospital. He re-planned the town centre in the late 1820s, with the intention of separating the Hospital from it and providing a grand approach to its gates. Supported by the Hospital's Secretary, Edward Hawke Locker (whose idea it was), Kay aimed to improve the 'circuitous, narrow and unsightly' road route from London, which was further blighted by an open-air market. His scheme cleared away the decayed post-medieval town that pressed up against the Hospital boundary, and replaced it with a formal layout of commercial streets around a new covered market, built in 1829–31.

The parades of stuccoed terraces in the centre of Greenwich were designed by Kay. He was also responsible for the elegant Trafalgar Tavern, whose cast-iron balconies, canopied bow-windows and an upper-storey loggia give fine views over the Thames. It was built on Royal Hospital land in 1837, replacing the old George tavern.

Hidden gem

A striking bronze statue of Lord Nelson (1758–1805) by Leslie Pover, 2005, stands outside the Trafalgar Tavern.

▶ *The Trafalgar Tavern, built in 1837, was celebrated for its whitebait suppers. This photograph was taken around 1915.*

Greenwich Fair

For over a hundred years Greenwich Fair was one of London's great popular attractions at Easter and Whitsuntide. The principal day-time amusement observed by the young Charles Dickens '[was] to drag young ladies up the steep hill which leads to the observatory, and then drag them down again, at the very top of their speed, greatly to the derangement of their curls and bonnet-caps' (from Sketches by Boz).

When night fell, the action moved to the town where itinerant theatres, menageries, objects of curiosity like dwarfs and giantesses, and a temporary ballroom, vied for the attention of enormous crowds. Such excess met opposition as the age became increasingly prim, and as annual numbers at the two fairs rose to about 250,000 with the coming of both steam ferries and trains to Greenwich in 1836–38. In 1857, after 30 years of complaint, respectable local residents succeeded in abolishing the Fair, which the Greenwich Free Press called, 'that old market of vice and debauchery'.

In the Town

Greenwich town centre is a unique part of London, with the covered Greenwich Market forming the focal point. There are also many other spots worth visiting, including several examples of fine achitecture.

Greenwich Market

 greenwichmarket.london

 10.00–17.30 Mon–Sun

 Free entry

Originally, Greenwich's covered market had three principal sections: meat, fish and vegetables. Above the colonnaded entrance from College Approach, there is still the original inscription: 'A False Balance is Abomination to the Lord but a Just Weight His Delight'. Turnpin Lane, at the south end of the Market, is the only surviving stretch of the town's narrow medieval alleys.

Today, the market houses around 120 different stalls and boutique shops, selling antiques and collectables, jewellery, photography, embroidery, arts and crafts. The present steel-framed roof replaced the original wooden one in 1908. In 2016, its covering had enlarged panels of tempered glass added, allowing natural light to flood in below, and a new food court and pavilion were opened for hungry visitors to sit and enjoy the street food on offer.

Did you know?

Nelson Road was the first part in Kay's improvement scheme. It replaced a solid block of old buildings with two formal stuccoed terraces. The north side centres round an archway into Greenwich Market. It also provided a long dramatic view down Romney Road toward St Alfege Church, which did not exist before.

St Alfege Church

 st-alfege.org.uk

 11.00/12.00–16.00 Tue-Sat, various services. Parish Eucharist 10.00 Sunday

 Free entry

Nicholas Hawksmoor's remarkable church of St Alfege is the architectural focus of Greenwich town. It was built between 1712 and 1718 to replace the medieval parish church, after its roof collapsed in 1710.

The first of the 'Fifty New Churches' in London ordered under Queen Anne, this Portland-stone cruciform church was designed by Hawksmoor. John James, his Clerk of Works at the Royal Hospital, re-cased the surviving medieval tower of St Alfege in 1730. The church's crypt was used by up to 40 families as an air-raid shelter during the Second World War, until March 1941 when the nave was destroyed by an incendiary bomb. The church's interior was later sensitively restored by Sir Albert Richardson, in 1953.

Hidden gem

The crypt is best known as the burial place of General James Wolfe, a British Army officer, primarily remembered for his capture of Quebec from the French in 1759, during the Seven Years War. The crypt was designed by Hawksmoor to be a space for the living, and possibly a school. Soon after the church was consecrated in 1718, the parishioners of Greenwich decided they had other plans. People paid to be buried in the crypt floor and, as a result, its current level is about three feet higher than originally. Wealthy local people – including the Wolfes – also set up family burial vaults in the crypt. There are over 1,000 bodies there, including John Julius Angerstein, founder of the National Gallery. The remains of Thomas Tallis, the great Tudor composer of church music, are believed to lie beneath the chancel.

◀ One of many post-war stained-glass windows in St Alfege Church. This one shows General James Wolfe.

St Alfege Church marks the spot where Vikings murdered Alfege, Archbishop of Canterbury, in 1012.

Did you know?

General James Wolfe was buried in the crypt on the evening of 20 November 1759. By coincidence, this was exactly as Admiral Hawke was defeating the French at the Battle of Quiberon Bay – the last triumph of the 'year of victories', in which Wolfe's capture of Quebec was another. Wolfe died leading his troops at Quebec, aged 32, and this is shown in a well-known painting by Edward Penny RA that forms part of his memorial in the church.

▲ *There has been a pathway at the side of the Church for centuries. Until 1938 it was called Church Passage.*

St Alfege Passage

This Passage holds a fine Georgian-style terrace, built 1844–51. The corner house on Church Street is one of five on its west side built sometime between 1690 and 1704. By 1800 this one was the Eight Bells tavern.

Greenwich Church Street

On the western side near St Alfege Church, numbers 15–21 are a group of modest houses with shops from about 1700, numbers 19 and 21 originally being one building. Numbers 15 and 17 are the taller and apparently earlier pair. Such late Stuart or early Georgian buildings are now very rare. Dr Johnson, the great English literary figure of the early to mid-18th century lived in Church Street after he first came to London in 1736.

Spread Eagle Yard

The Eagle was an 18th-century coaching inn when the corner on which it stands on Nevada Street was on the main road east out of Greenwich. The archway into the vanished stable yard was built about 1780.

▲ *The archway into Spread Eagle Yard can be found on the corner of Nevada Street, which was formerly known as Silver Street. The lively Greenwich Theatre, on the site of an earlier music hall, is on the opposite corner.*

The Fan Museum

🌐 thefanmuseum.org.uk

🕐 11.00–17.00 Wed–Sat

🎫 Charged admission

Located in two beautifully restored Grade II-listed Georgian town houses, designed by John Savery in 1721, The Fan Museum is the world's first museum dedicated to the history of fans and craft of fan making. The renowned collection of fans and fan leaves is comprehensive and the elegant Orangery at the rear includes fine murals by Jane Barraclough.

▶ *The permanent display within the Museum offers an introduction to fans, and the upstairs gallery holds exhibitions.*

◀ *3-in-1 folding fan, France, 2007. Crafted by contemporary fan maker, Sylvain Le Guen & based on the Matryoshka Russian doll concept. The Fan Museum, Helene Alexander Collection.*

Devonport House and Hospital Burial Ground

Built by Sir Edwin Cooper as a nurses' home in 1924–34, on the site of the second Greenwich Hospital burial ground, Devonport House incorporates two-thirds of William Newton's Greenwich Hospital School building of 1783–84 as a rear wing. It is now partly a student residence.

The cemetery was closed in 1857 but Thomas Ripley's officers' mausoleum of 1750 and some graves around it remain. Captain Hardy of the *Victory*, later Governor of the Hospital, 1834–39, is one of many distinguished officers buried in the vault. Nelson's servant, Tom Allen, lies in a marked grave nearby.

Greenwich Foot Tunnel

Built by Alexander Binnie for the London County Council in 1900–02, originally for workers from south of the river to reach the London Docks, the double entrance to the tunnel has circular red-brick panelling with a domed glass roof.

▼ *The earliest part of Devonport House was constructed in 1782–84 as enlarged new premises for the Greenwich Hospital School.*

Hidden gem

It is worth going through the tile-glazed foot tunnel for the 'Canaletto' view of Greenwich from Island Gardens, north of the river (see photo above and pages 8–9).

Greenwich Pier

The Pier was originally constructed in 1836 for the growing steamer traffic, and the river is still a major route for visitors to Greenwich by the frequent boat services. The new Pier buildings were constructed in 2011–12.

Greenwich Railway Station

The London and Greenwich Railway was the world's first suburban line, built in 1836–38. It runs from London Bridge on a viaduct that may be the world's largest solid brick structure and, incidentally, gives a fine view of Thomas Archer's wonderful church of St Paul's Deptford which, like St Alfege Church, was one of Queen Anne's 'Fifty New Churches'. The handsome station, built by George Smith in 1840, and rebuilt in 1878, originally had a high-level platform, lowered when the line

▲ *Travel by river remains one of the best ways to reach Greenwich. Island Gardens are on the left.*

was put in a cut-and-cover tunnel to run east beyond Greenwich in 1878. It is now also a DLR interchange.

Trafalgar Quarters

This handsome brick building, colonnaded and arcaded to the ground floor, was constructed in 1813 by John Yenn as offices for administering the finances and out-pensions of the Royal Hospital. Over the central bays is the finely carved Hospital coat of arms. It is flanked by lodges of contemporary date, although the upper level and distinctive oriel window to the north lodge were added about 1900. It is now run by Greenwich Hospital as sheltered accommodation.

▼ *Trafalgar Quarters, built in 1813, are now Grade II listed. They were originally offices for Greenwich Hospital.*

Trinity Laban Conservatoire of Music & Dance

 trinitylaban.ac.uk

 Varied programme, see trinitylaban.ac.uk/whats-on

 Event prices vary, many are free

Trinity Laban was created in 2005, when two leading institutions – Trinity College of Music and the Laban Centre – came together to form the UK's first conservatoire of music and dance. The institution has cultivated an international reputation as a centre of excellence, offering world-class training in dance, music and musical theatre.

Enjoy Choral Evensong on Mondays at 17.30 and Sung Eucharists on Sundays at 11.00 performed by The Old Royal Naval College Trinity Laban Chapel Choir. The Old Royal Naval College Chapel also hosts student ensembles in lunchtime concerts on Tuesdays and Fridays during term-time.

Hidden gem

Trinity Laban puts on 350+ performances, festivals and masterclasses each year. Visitors can also sit in the courtyard and listen to the music spilling out from the practice rooms for free.

In the Park

The Park still has some of the strong formal lines of its 17th-century layout, but overall it is more a landscaped park of the 18th century. It has been open to the public since about 1705 but only on a regular basis from the 1830s. Set around the Park are some of the best surviving examples in London of affluent private houses of the 17th to 19th centuries. Within it there are various monuments and buildings of note, as well as Roman and Anglo-Saxon remains. Among the trees, the great chestnuts, some dating from the 1660s layout, are especially fine.

Greenwich Hill has always offered excellent views of the historic buildings below it and of distant London. Many artists have taken advantage of this. Well-known 17th-century views by Danckerts and Vorsterman were followed in 1809 by the greatest of English landscape and marine painters,

J.M.W. Turner, and by later 19th-century recorders of both the landscape and the Park social scene. Westwards the eye is led along the Thames towards the dome of Sir Christopher Wren's St Paul's Cathedral – a view legally protected from obstruction by the spread of ever-taller modern buildings. East and north lie surviving points of river-based industry and the O2 (the former Millennium Dome). In front, the cluster of large, modern Docklands buildings has grown ever-denser around Cesar Pelli's Canary Wharf tower (1 Canada Square), completed in 1991.

There are numerous interesting structures and monuments in the Park, including the octagonal bandstand, the delightful teahouse of 1906–07 and on the hill near the Anglo-Saxon barrows, an abstract bronze statue called *Standing Figure: Knife Edge*, by the sculptor Henry Moore.

Anglo-Saxon barrow cemetery

This ancient burial ground includes at least 31 barrows dating from the 6th to 8th centuries AD. Several were opened in 1714 by the Park Keeper, and others in 1784. Human hair, glass beads, cloth and flints were among the finds.

The Queen's Orchard

The Park's walled former 'Dwarf Orchard' is the last survivor of three 17th-century tree nurseries along its northern edge. Recently taken back into Park management and replanted with fruit trees as the Greenwich Park Orchard, it is largely maintained by volunteers with limited general access.

Conduit House

This small red-brick building on the Park's lower slopes near Croom's Hill has plaques on its south façade

▲ *Conduit houses are now rare buildings, related to the pre-modern water supply from local springs.*

that read 'Greenwich Hospital' and 'Standard Reservoir'. Marking the end of a long water conduit, it appears to have been erected about 1700 in connection with the building of the Hospital, probably under the direction of Nicholas Hawksmoor, as part of the modernisation of the water-supply system that had served the Tudor palace.

St Mary's Lodge

Built about 1823, this stuccoed cottage, designed by John Nash as an Italianate version of a picturesque estate lodge, stands in the north-west corner of the

Park, near St Mary's Gate. It is now a café, with a pleasant garden area. The lodge and the fine wrought-iron St Mary's Gate to the Park take their name from the church (1823–1936) that occupied the site of the nearby King William statue, and were built at the same time.

Statue of General Wolfe

Robert Tait McKenzie's 1930 bronze statue of Major-General James Wolfe stands at the top of Greenwich Hill. Wolfe (1727–59) was a resident of Greenwich and commanded the British forces at the capture of Quebec, where he and his opponent, the Marquis de Montcalm were both killed. Wolfe is buried in St Alfege Church, Greenwich. The statue was a gift from the Canadian people.

Statue of William IV

Now the centrepiece of the south entrance to the National Maritime Museum, Samuel Nixon's granite statue of King William IV was erected in King William Street at the City end of London Bridge in 1844. Called the 'Sailor King' from his early career in the navy (including under Nelson), William reigned from 1830 to 1837. The statue was moved to Greenwich in 1936 owing to City road improvements.

▲ *The statue of Major-General James Wolfe stands at the top of Greenwich Hill.*

▲ *The impressive granite statue of William IV, near the National Maritime Museum.*

▲ *Blackheath Gate Lodge is set just outside the gates of Greenwich Park.*

Blackheath Gate Lodge
Built by John Phipps, 1851–52, this is a remarkably early and robust example of the Domestic Revival style. It was built to house the Park Keeper as part of a campaign of improvements to extend public access.

Bandstand
Built around 1880, this pagoda-like octagonal bandstand has cast-iron columns with decorative spandrels which support a conical copper roof. It is used for regular summer concerts.

Queen Elizabeth's Oak
This 12th-century oak, dead for over 100 years and now fallen, was associated with Henry VIII and Elizabeth I.

Park's borders
Set around the Park's borders are some of the best surviving examples and finest concentrations of historic private houses in London. Croom's Hill, the ancient route to Greenwich from Blackheath, is on the western border of the Park; Maze Hill borders the east, with Park Vista to the north.

Macartney House
Home of General Wolfe and his parents from 1752, this dates from the 17th century with later extensions, including by Sir John Soane, 1802. In a letter of 1751 Wolfe referred to it as 'the prettiest-situated house in England'. On Chesterfield Walk, backing onto the west wall of the Park, it has a commemorative blue plaque to Wolfe on the Park side.

▲ *The bandstand in the Park hosts concerts and other performances in the summer.*

▲ *Macartney House, formerly the Wolfe family home, dates from the 17th century.*

Ranger's House

This classical building was built about 1700 for Admiral Francis Hosier, best remembered by a ballad (*Admiral Hosier's Ghost*), which marked his death from fever in the West Indies. The writer and statesman 4th Earl of Chesterfield, who later lived here, built the south gallery, with a north wing added by 1794. In 1815 it became the 'grace and favour' residence of the Ranger of Greenwich Park. Now run by English Heritage, it holds the spectacular Wernher Collection of fine and decorative art, much of which dates back to the Renaissance.

Further down Croom's Hill are late-17th- and early 18th-century houses and terraces, though some may be more ancient behind the facades. The Manor House (c.1700) near the top is particularly fine, and the 18th-century Grange (no. 52) has a splendid garden-wall gazebo overlooking the Park. This was designed by Robert Hooke in 1672 for the owner, Sir William Hooker, Sheriff and later Lord Mayor of London. The neo-Gothic Roman Catholic Church of Our Lady Star of the Sea is the most imposing building on Croom's Hill and was built of ragstone in 1851 to the designs of William Wardell, later an important architect in Australia. The chancel and chapel of St Joseph were decorated by A.W.N. Pugin and the Lady Chapel by E.W. Pugin.

Brick-gabled Heathgate House (no. 66), of about 1630, is the oldest in Greenwich, completed even before the Queen's House.

▲ *Ranger's House seen from the Park. The 4th Earl of Chesterfield, who lived there between 1749 and 1773, later added the south gallery on the left.*

▲ *Vanbrugh Castle is the only survivor of a group of houses that Sir John Vanbrugh built for his family.*

Vanbrugh Castle

Begun in 1718, Vanbrugh Castle on Maze Hill, to the east of the Park, was built by the architect and playwright Sir John Vanbrugh as his own residence while he was Surveyor to the Royal Hospital for Seamen, and is believed to be the first example of a private house consciously designed to emulate the style of the Middle Ages.

Nos. 32–40, Maze Hill

Built by Daniel Asher Alexander in 1807–12 as the infirmary of the Royal Naval Asylum. They stand on the Royal Hospital's first burial ground, of which the enclosing walls and officers' mausoleum vault survive.

Park Vista

On the northern boundary of the Park, houses on Park Vista include the last standing remnant of the Tudor palace, a conduit house of about 1515 bearing the arms of Henry VIII. This is now part of a group of 17th- to 19th-century houses: The Chantry, (no. 34) and St Alfege Vicarage (no. 33). The Manor House (no. 13) is an attractive early 18th-century Georgian building with an unusual weather-boarded belvedere overlooking the Park. Hamilton House and Park Place (nos. 15–18) date from the late 18th century, while nos. 1–12 also form a handsome terrace of the early 19th century.

Trinity Hospital

East of the town centre on the river walk, Trinity Hospital is an almshouse founded in 1613 by Henry Howard, Earl of Northampton. The present Gothic remodelling dates to 1812. Beyond the large Greenwich Power Station, 1902–10, Ballast Quay is an attractive river frontage of early 19th-century houses. The view east to Blackwall Point and the O2 takes in Enderby Wharf, the base from 1834 of the Enderby family's South Sea whaling fleet.

▲ *The Trinity Hospital almshouses, founded in 1613, still operate today as accommodation for elderly residents of reduced financial circumstances.*

▲ *Greenwich Park in spring.*

Top 10 tips for a day trip

1 Stand on the world-famous Meridian Line
◉ **Royal Observatory, Meridian Line**
You can't come to Greenwich without getting a photo of yourself standing on the Prime Meridian of the World at the Royal Observatory – the home of Greenwich Mean Time (GMT).

2 Touch the hull of *Cutty Sark*
◉ *Cutty Sark*
Don't miss the chance to visit the world's last surviving tea clipper. This award-winning 19th-century sailing ship, raised over three metres, offers you the jaw-dropping experience of walking directly underneath its keel.

3 See a show at London's only planetarium
◉ **Royal Observatory, Planetarium & Astronomy Centre**
Think of the Peter Harrison Planetarium as a tour bus of the Universe, taking you on amazing journeys to explore and experience the wonders of the night sky – with commentary by expert astronomers from the Royal Observatory.

4 Visit some of the finest art and architecture in the UK
◉ **The Queen's House**
The Queen's House is the first example of classical architecture in the UK. It is also home to the iconic 'Armada Portrait' of Queen Elizabeth I, which is on free public display.

5 Explore the magnificent Painted Hall and Chapel
◉ **Old Royal Naval College**
Admire the spectacular symmetry of these unique buildings, designed by Sir Christopher Wren, including James Thornhill's magnificent Painted Hall (1708–26) and James 'Athenian' Stuart's Greek-revival chapel (1789). Pop into the Visitor Centre to find out more about the Maritime Greenwich World Heritage Site.

6 Visit the only museum in the UK devoted to the history of fans
◉ **The Fan Museum**
Explore this collection of fans with examples from all over the world, from the 12th century to the present day. The collection is particularly strong in 18th and 19th century European fans. It's quite literally fan-tastic and definitely worth a visit!

7 Enjoy some excellent shopping and street food
◉ **Greenwich Market**
Widely regarded as one of London's best markets, there are over 120 arts, craft and antique stalls so you can browse everything from hand-crafted toys to boutique fashion and jewellery, before you reward yourself with some delicious international food from a range of stalls.

8 Enjoy a stroll through tranquil flower, herb and orchard gardens
◉ **Greenwich Park**
Greenwich Park is the oldest of London's royal parks. Formerly a hunting

park for Henry VIII, it covers 183 acres (74 hectares), including traces from Roman and Saxon times. There's a boating lake and a bandstand, as well as some hidden treasures!

9 Explore Britain's extensive maritime history
⊙ **National Maritime Museum**
Uncover stories of adventure and piracy, ambition and greed in the 'Tudor and Stuart Seafarers' gallery, or visit 'Polar Worlds' to discover tales of Arctic and Antarctic exploration.

10 Hop on a river cruise at Greenwich Pier
⊙ **King William Walk**
Did you know the River Thames is 215 miles long? You won't be able to cruise the full length in a day but could certainly take in some of its finest city sights. Cruises depart every 40 minutes from Westminster Pier, London Eye Pier, Tower Pier and Greenwich Pier every day of the year (except Christmas Day). Greenwich is just 20 minutes from Central London.

Family activities

Greenwich has plenty to offer families. Here are our suggestions for a top day out with the kids.

See a special under-7s show at the Peter Harrison Planetarium
◎ **Royal Observatory, Planetarium & Astronomy Centre**
A visit to the Peter Harrison Planetarium can fly you into the heart of the Sun, transport you to distant galaxies, show you the birth of a star or land you on Mars. Visit rmg.co.uk/whats-on/planetarium-shows for full details of shows available for under-7s.

Touch a 4.5 billion-year-old meteorite
◎ **Royal Observatory, Planetarium & Astronomy Centre**
The Gibeon Meteorite, on display in the Astronomy Centre at the Royal Observatory, is as old as the Earth and the Sun, and you're welcome to touch!

Take part in *Cutty Sark* games and interactives
◎ *Cutty Sark*
There are several games and interactive displays on board the *Cutty Sark* to help children learn about the ship's fascinating history.

Climb into *Cutty Sark*'s bunk beds and explore the Captain's cabin
◎ *Cutty Sark*
Go aboard *Cutty Sark* and discover where the crew ate and slept. Kids can explore the captain's quarters or climb into the bunk beds used by the seamen.

AHOY! Children's Gallery for children up to 7
◎ **National Maritime Museum**
Take toddlers and young children to visit the AHOY! Children's Gallery. Polar exploration, pirates and a host of other maritime themes are brought to life in this playful and immersive space.

All Hands Children's Gallery for 6–12 year olds
◎ **National Maritime Museum**
Older children can visit the All Hands Children's Gallery, where they can dress up as sailors, practise Morse code and load cargo onto a ship with a crane.

Journey across the Great Map
◎ **National Maritime Museum**
Take children of any age to visit the Great Map at the centre of the Museum, where they can walk across the world and explore different continents. Accompanying adults can refuel at the adjacent café.

Greenwich Park Boating Pond
◎ **Greenwich Park, north-east corner**
Outdoor fun for the whole family to enjoy, with a fleet of 5-person pedaloes and 2-person pedal boats, ready to set sail. There is also an adventure playground for 3–13 year olds (free entry; spring-summer only).

Where to eat

Greenwich caters for a diverse range of tastes and budgets. A selection to suit all tastes is listed below.

Astronomy Café and Terrace
◎ **Royal Observatory Greenwich, The Avenue**
A relaxed spot to enjoy a light lunch: includes hot and cold drinks, cakes, hearty soups and fresh salads.

Cutty Sark Café
◎ *Cutty Sark* **(open to ticket holders only)**
Served beneath the historic vessel's hull, afternoon tea here is a real treat. The café also serves sandwiches and light meals.

Cutty Sark Pub
◎ **4–6 Ballast Quay**
Over 200 years old, this pub serves seasonal British dishes.

Sticks'n'Sushi
◎ **1 Nelson Road**
This Japanese restaurant serves sushi, grilled food and salads.

Greenwich Market
◎ **Greenwich Market**
There are over 40 different street food stalls offering cuisine from around the world.

The Mitre
◎ **291 Greenwich High Road**
Flavoursome food, a diverse drinks menu and an authentic, homely atmosphere to suit all occasions.

The Old Brewery
◎ **The Pepys Building, Old Royal Naval College**
This pub has an impressive dining room as well as an expansive outdoor terrace. The perfect spot for a refreshing summer drink and bite to eat.

Paul Rhodes Bakery
◎ **37 King William Walk**
Independent bakery serving freshly baked bread, cakes and pastries.

Parkside Café and Terrace
◎ **National Maritime Museum**
Enjoy award-winning coffee, maritime-themed dishes and seasonal cocktails while looking out over Greenwich Park. Located in the Sammy Ofer Wing of the Museum.

Pavilion Café
◎ **Blackheath Avenue**
Situated at the top of the hill in Greenwich Park, near the Observatory. Offers a range of freshly made dishes in a cosy setting.

Richard I
◎ **52/54 Royal Hill**
A relaxing drinking and dining space, with a large, open garden.

The Sail Loft
◎ **11 Victoria Parade**
Right on the river, west of Greenwich Pier, this pub serves up fresh food and drinks with a side order of wonderful views.

Trafalgar Tavern
◎ **Park Row**
Serving traditional British dishes in a handsome riverside building that has been a well-known Greenwich venue since it was built in 1837.

How to get here

Greenwich is just 20 minutes from central London. It's easy to get here by train, DLR or boat. For Greenwich town centre, the nearest stations are:
- Cutty Sark DLR
- Greenwich rail station and Maze Hill rail station
- Greenwich Pier

You can reach Greenwich from central London by direct rail routes from Cannon Street and London Bridge, or DLR from Bank. By London Underground Jubilee Line, change at Canary Wharf for the DLR at Heron Quays.

One of the best ways to arrive is by river. Regular riverboat services run to Greenwich Pier from Westminster, Embankment, London Bridge City, Canary Wharf and Tower Piers.

The following buses stop near the National Maritime Museum and Queen's House: 129, 177, 180, 188, 286, 386 and N1.

For *Cutty Sark*: 129, 177, 180, 188, 199 and 386.

For the Royal Observatory and Peter Harrison Planetarium: 53, 54, 202 and 380.

Greenwich town centre

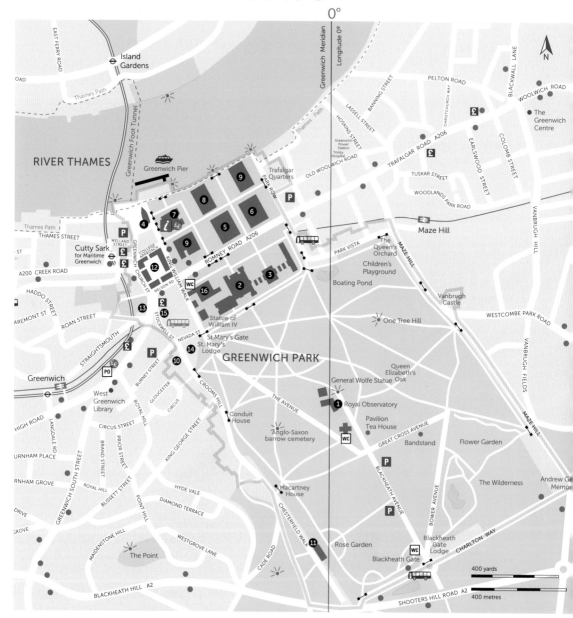

0°

RIVER THAMES

Island Gardens

Greenwich Meridian Longitude 0°

Greenwich Foot Tunnel

Thames Path

EAST FERRY ROAD

Greenwich Pier

Trafalgar Quarters

PARK ROW

PELTON ROAD

BANNING STREET

LASSELL STREET

HOSKINS STREET

CHRISTCHURCH WAY

Greenwich Power Station Trinity Hospital

OLD WOOLWICH ROAD

TRAFALGAR ROAD A206

TUSKAR STREET

WOODLANDS PARK ROAD

The Greenwich Centre

BLACKWALL LANE

WOOLWICH ROAD

COLOMA STREET

EARLSWOOD STREET

PARK VISTA

Maze Hill

VANBRUGH HILL

THAMES STREET

Cutty Sark for Maritime Greenwich

WELLAND STREET

GREENWICH CHURCH ST

COLLEGE APPROACH

KING WILLIAM WALK

NELSON RD

ROMNEY ROAD A206

The Queen's Orchard

Children's Playground

Boating Pond

One Tree Hill

Vanbrugh Castle

WESTCOMBE PARK ROAD

VANBRUGH FIELDS

Statue of William IV

St Mary's Gate St. Mary's Lodge

NEVADA ST

STOCKWELL ST

GREENWICH PARK

Queen Elizabeth's Oak

General Wolfe Statue

MAZE HILL

Greenwich

West Greenwich Library

STRAIGHTSMOUTH

BURNEY STREET

ROYAL HILL

GLOUCESTER CIRCUS

CROOMS HILL

Conduit House

Anglo-Saxon barrow cemetery

THE AVENUE

Royal Observatory

Pavilion Tea House

GREAT CROSS AVENUE

Bandstand

Flower Garden

The Wilderness

Andrew G Memo

HIGH ROAD

LANGDALE RD

BRAND STREET

PRIOR STREET

CIRCUS STREET

KING GEORGE STREET

Macartney House

BLACKHEATH AVENUE

BOWER AVENUE

CHARLTON WAY

HADDO STREET

ROAN STREET

CLAREMONT ST

A200 CREEK ROAD

ST

ROYAL HILL

BLISSETT STREET

POINT HILL

HYDE VALE

DIAMOND TERRACE

CHESTERFIELD WALK

CADE ROAD

Rose Garden

Blackheath Gate Lodge

Blackheath Gate

URNHAM PLACE

RNHAM GROVE

DRIVE

GROVE

GREENWICH SOUTH STREET

MAIDSTONE HILL

The Point

WESTGROVE LANE

BLACKHEATH HILL A2

SHOOTERS HILL ROAD A2

400 yards

400 metres

visitgreenwich
time after time